JENNY I
life, ever
read. She
and pape
pictures
married

grew up and went to school in Wimbledon before going on to study dress design at Kingston College of Art. After a brief spell as a model she joined the International Publishing Corporation as a fashion editor. She gave up her career long ago to bring up her two daughters and to spend more time restoring the old Victorian house near Kew Gardens where she has lived for the last thirty years. She is a natural 'handyman' and in her element sawing, hammering, painting, planning and planting gardens and now that her daughters are grown up, she finds herself writing again.

Is Anybody There?

Jenny Deane

SilverWood

Published in 2022 by SilverWood Books

SilverWood Books Ltd
14 Small Street, Bristol, BS1 1DE, United Kingdom
www.silverwoodbooks.co.uk

Copyright © Jenny Deane 2022
Author photograph © Westend Portraits 2022

The right of Jenny Deane to be identified as the author of this work has been asserted in accordance with the Copyright, Designs and Patents Act 1988 Sections 77 and 78.

All rights reserved. No part of this publication may be reproduced, stored in a retrieval system, or transmitted in any form or by any means, electronic, mechanical, photocopying, recording or otherwise, without prior permission of the copyright holder.

This is a work of fiction. Names, characters, places and incidents either are products of the author's imagination or are used fictitiously. Any resemblance to actual events or locales or persons, living or dead, is entirely coincidental.

ISBN 978-1-80042-173-8 (paperback)
ISBN 978-1-80042-174-5 (ebook)

British Library Cataloguing in Publication Data
A CIP catalogue record for this book is
available from the British Library

Page design and typesetting by SilverWood Books

For those I love and who persuaded me to publish this book

Contents

LOVE 13

- The Morning Bell — 15
- The Affair — 16
- Blossom — 17
- Love Lost — 18
- For Ian — 19
- Tears — 20
- Richmond Park — 21
- Why? — 22
- Lost Love — 23
- The Kiss — 24
- Disillusion — 25
- Obsession — 26

HUMOUR 27

- The Trouble With… — 29
- A Misunderstanding — 30
- Lies — 31
- Jane — 32

Red	33
My Brother's Wife	34
A Brief Affair	35
The Unsuccessful Ghost	36
What's in a Name?	37
Directions	38
The Prankster	39
From a Stranger to a Friend in 8 Easy Steps	40
An Alternative Life	41
The Party	42
Tulips	43
A Nonsense Rhyme	44
Tomorrow is Another Day	45

WAR   47

Whitehall 2013	49
David	50
When All Is Said and Done	51
The Tower of London 2014	52
After the Battle	53
Retreat	54

"Mother"	55
The Suitcase	56

SEASONS   57

September	59
Mist	60
The Frost Fairy	61
Autumn	62
Sun and Moon – A Love Affair	64
The North Coast of Denmark	65
Not Knowing	66
Rain	67
Winter	68
Summer	69

LOSS   71

Do Not Lay Me In a Dark Place	73
Near Death Experience	74
Sitting in the Theatre 27 April 2016	75
I Have Lost My Child	76
Download to Oblivion	77
On the Loss of a Child	78

Only the Things I Didn't Do	79
If I Should Die Tonight	80
Friendship Lost	81

LIMERICKS   83

Limerick	85
Limerick	86
Limerick	87
Limerick	88
Limerick	89
Limerick	90

MISCELLANEOUS   91

The Gift	93
Waiting at the Eurostar Terminus	94
1963	95
Despair 1750	96
Despair 2020	97
Good God!	98
Stranger Danger	99
I Am Called to the Sea	100
Fear	101

Waiting	102
Tell Me the Truth	103
On First Hearing Mahler's Symphony No. 5	104
Mermaids	105
Where I Belong	106
Analysis of Friendship	107
?	108
I Am Afraid of the Night	109
Coronavirus	110
Has Anybody Seen My Mind?	111
Christmas 2020	112
After Dickens	113
"Forbidden"	114
"Oh Come All Ye Faithfull"	116
Belonging	117
A Storm	118
The Man I Used To Be	119
The Devil You Know	120
When I Write in the Night	121
Acknowledgements	123

LOVE

The Morning Bell

Goodnight my love, sleep well
Until the morning bell;
And when it tolls remember me
Who loved you best, but set you free
To turn unto another love
Who loved you less, but you did see
In him what you found not in me.
Remember how we shared the hours
On grassy banks amid the flowers,
As each to each our kisses sweet
Did somehow make our love complete.
How gentle was the evening sun,
How timeless our love, fresh begun.
Yet now I find I am set free
And you hear not my empty plea,
For now when tolls the morning bell
I only hear love's deathly knell.

The Affair

Beside me my bed is empty, cold.
He is gone.
Gone away to that other bed,
Where he belongs.
For a few brief hours he was mine
And I was happy.
But what draws him away?
Are those other bonds so strong?
Unbreakable in fact?
For here I am, alone again and weep
And yet, just for a while,
My love was mine.

Blossom

Against the morning sky
The blossom shines,
Dew-drop fresh and pink as Mary's cheeks.
Sweet Mary in her shiny summer dress
Dappled beneath the blossom,
Her legs crossed carelessly upon the grass,
Her hand in mine.
We lie together, silent, knowing surely it will fade
And we must part.
But in her gentle touch I am content
That for this golden moment she is mine;
Her perfect cheeks, her smile, her soft blue eyes
Belong to me,
Until the blossom fades.

Love Lost

Where did those days of long-lost summer go
Those days of kisses, sweet as summer wine,
When you and I together faced the world
And thought that we could halt the rush of time?

Your nut-brown summer skin upon the grass,
Your tender smile beneath a golden sky
Held me in thrall, I dreamed of nothing more,
And thought that should I lose you I would die.

Yet in the rush of time you slipped away,
Silent as death, for death it was to me.
For I believed those summer promises
And now your shadow will not set me free.

For Ian

When we were young and strong
And full of joy,
Careless with youth
And unaware of change;
We shared so much,
Such comfortable love.
Yet we are to each other
As we always were.
We talk
As we have always done,
Hold hands
As ever we used to do.
The love we have
Unchanged – unchangeable.

Tears

My tears fall slowly, heavy,
Like the first drops of rain
Before a thunderstorm.
My heart is breaking slowly too.
The pain tight
Like the string of a guitar.
No one told me,
When I gave my heart away
The pain would be so great, so absolute,
I did not know.

Richmond Park

Regret would be if we had never met,
Nor bound ourselves together in the dark,
Nor found within ourselves those deeper things
We sought, but found not when we were apart.

Regret would be if we had never kissed,
Nor held each other till the morning lark
Rose from the earth in ever richer song
Above the shining plain of Richmond Park.

Why?

I forgot – to ask
And am left with the burning question
Why did you go?
Was the fault mine – all along?
Did I say something, do something
Which made you unhappy?
Did I not take enough care,
Of your feelings?
Should I have listened more
Talked less?
Given you more space?
I thought we had everything, you and I
That we were happy.
Maybe I expected too much,
But you said nothing.
And now, all I know is that you are gone
And I will be forever left wondering,
Why?

Lost Love

Simple hours of simple joy
I shared with you today.
I would ask more, but you'd refuse
And send me on my way.

"Tomorrow," you might say, and then
You'd walk away, alone,
And I'd be left still wondering
Just why you might have gone.

I thought it would be fun at first
To dally for a while,
But then my heart became involved,
Won over by your smile.

"I am not ready," you would say,
"To fall in love again"
And yet I dreamed you'd learn to love,
And hoped, despite the pain.

But I was foolish, hoping still,
For I knew from the start
That you would walk away from me,
That we were bound to part.

And so I had to let you go
And follow not this time
For I knew we could not go back,
You never would be mine.

The Kiss

Of all the dreams in all the world
My greatest dream is this,
That should I meet you suddenly
You'd promise me a kiss.

I'd ask for nothing in return,
No promised wedding ring,
I'd be content with that one kiss.
It would mean everything.

And should we, one day, meet again,
You old and grey and sad,
I'd smile and greet you as a friend
But for that kiss be glad.

Disillusion

I thought I loved you,
All the signs were there;
How I caught my breath
When your hand, so gently,
Touched mine.
How my pulse raced
When you smiled at me.
They told me it was love
And I believed them.

At a later date
(Too late in fact)
I realised the truth.
My madly beating heart
A medical condition,
An accident of nature
I was told.
And the smile I thought so warm
When we first met
A dental misalignment,
Nothing more.

As it turns out
It was an easy mistake to make.
But had I been a medical man
And not a fool,
I might have known.

Obsession

Did you not know how I loved you?
Did you not see?
Did you not notice how I trembled
When our fingers touched?
And yet I dared not say
For fear of what – rejection?
Others have loved me
Have held me in their arms,
Have whispered promises of love.
And I have tried so hard
To capture what I miss,
Yet somehow I cannot.
I thought one day that you must see,
Must realise,
Must hear the frantic beating of my heart.
Yet still I had not courage for the words
So I whispered them silently, under my breath
Hoping.

HUMOUR

The Trouble With…

The trouble with trouble
It often comes double.
You think you can't beat it
Completely defeat it,
But life's more confusing
And far less amusing.
It seems somehow appalling
When trouble comes calling.
If you can learn to destroy it,
Somehow, re-deploy it
And send it away
For another dark day;
Dismember its parts
And ignore all its arts,
Then the trouble is gone
And your misery done.
So try hard to avoid strife
Just relax and enjoy life.

A Misunderstanding

Just down the street, one bright and sunny day,
I met a man who told me he was gay.
But I misunderstood that he was gay
In quite another way than I had thought,
Or even dared to say.
So as we parted, each to his own way,
I felt that it was up to me to say, quite happily to him,
I too was gay.

Lies

I had a friend called Sammy Blue
Who told me things that weren't quite true,
And when I asked him why he lied
He looked at me with eyes quite wide
And said, "Well, telling lies is fun,
So I tell lies to everyone,
And no one seems to mind too much
They give a more exotic touch.
It's far more fun to tell a lie
And really easy once you try."

Jane

Jane was a mistake, her mother said
One night of lust in that damn bed.
If she'd had just one glass of wine,
With that alone she'd have been fine.
But no, he'd topped her up again,
He'd told her she'd be right as rain.
And now, at ten years down the line,
She knew that she was far from fine.
She'd had ambition once – and plans,
She'd even dreamt of marriage bans.
But then came Jane, out of the blue,
What all her friends had said was true.
"She'll tie you down, just wait and see
Once you're a mum you're never free."
And having Jane HAD held her back,
She should have had a better crack
At life she felt, which had been fine
Until that second glass of wine.

Red

I should have bought that dress
"Too red," you said.
I "would have looked a mess,"
You said.
But I like red, and in my head
I thought it would impress.

My Brother's Wife

To tell the truth, I do not like her much,
My brother's wife.
Her hair too red
Her nails too long,
Her perfume just a bit too strong.
Her skirt too short,
Her heels too high,
With just a little too much thigh.
Her top too low
(Despite the bow)
Thus leaving far too much on show.
And in a crowd
Her voice too loud,
She's far too arrogant and proud.
So even though she's full of life,
She really isn't very nice
My brother's wife.

A Brief Affair

I never thought that I'd get caught,
Never a part of my plan
The situation seemed too fraught
To bother with a man.

But somehow, on a rainy day,
My resolution failed
This real good-looker came along
And all objections paled.

But when at last the sun came out,
And I could see more clearly
I realised he was just a lout
I didn't like him really.

I said "Farewell," with little grace,
So glad to have him gone
And now I can't recall his face.
He wasn't even fun.

The Unsuccessful Ghost

I tried, I really tried, to no avail.
I wrapped myself in sheets, I went quite pale.
I moaned and groaned, I even wailed,
But obviously I badly failed.
I even walked right through a door,
I banged my head. It's really sore.
The children all just stood and stared
I don't think they were really scared.
Perhaps I wasn't really dead,
I'll try a new career instead.

What's in a Name?

My name is Jane. It's such a shame
I'd rather have been called Elaine.
I'm Jane, with spots and curly hair,
Elaine would have long legs, be fair.
She'd have blue eyes and cupid lips
And not have forty-two inch hips.
Elaine would talk like Princess Anne
And even though I'm not a fan
It would be nice to meet smart faces
Go to some exciting places.
I'd wear short skirts and thigh-high boots
Or spend my life in City suits.
My friends say, "Jane, it's just a name,"
But still I'd rather be Elaine.

Directions

The other day I met a stranger
And asked him the way into town.
He told me to go in the other direction
And to take the road going down.
When I got to the bottom I came to a junction
And didn't know which way to go,
But a woman said, "Follow the road to the left
Where you'll see a large sign saying 'slow'.
If you turn at that corner you'll come to a square,
Go on past a pub called 'The Queen'
There's a bus stop outside where the schoolchildren meet
And a road which leads onto the green.
At the green turn around and go back up the hill
Till you come to the old covered market."
So I did what she said and in no time at all
I ended up where I had started.

The Prankster

He'd been a prankster all his life.
'Twas very hard on his poor wife.
As he set off she watched in vain
His leaving in the pouring rain
In swimming trunks and aqualung,
Pretending he was having fun.
And as the local children laughed
And pointed at him running past,
He rattled his collection tin
And hoped they'd all put something in.

From a Stranger to a Friend in 8 Easy Steps

I remember a meeting once
With a man I didn't know.
He showed me the way to the station
Which was where I wanted to go.
We travelled together to Vauxhall,
We walked with him holding my hand,
How we ended up in bed together
I really don't quite understand.

An Alternative Life

Sixty-five years is far too long
To sit upon a throne,
Especially when one stops to think
Of all one might have done.
I don't much care for dressing up,
Tiaras in my hair,
And all those jewels weigh me down,
I simply do not care.
I'd gladly live in brogues and tweeds,
A scarf around my head,
That's really all a person needs
If one's to look well-bred.
I'd spend my days astride a horse,
The corgis as my heels,
A better way to get about
Than bumpy carriage wheels.
No one to tell me what to do,
Each day would be my own,
To know I could do what I like
Forget about my throne.
It's nice sometimes to sit and dream
And think of who one might have been
If not the Queen.

The Party

I think I have most of the social graces,
I simply don't remember names, or faces,
I shake hands, smile and start a conversation.
"How nice to meet you.
Have we met before?"
And, "Was your journey easy from the station?"
"Hello Joanne, you're looking very well.
It's been five years. I really couldn't tell."
Oh Lord, he knows me. Now what do I do?
I should remember, yet I've not a clue.
I sip a drink and hesitate a while.
I force myself to imitate a smile.
Oh please could someone come to rescue me.
I'm simply too embarrassed now to flee.
We talk a lot,
It's far too hot
My face is flushed I know.
My instinct tells me strongly now
It's time for me to go.
I've drunk too much, I leave too late,
And then he asks me on a date.
Mistakenly, we kiss at the front door
And who is he? I'm really still not sure.

Tulips

I don't like tulips very much
They're far too stiff and far too Dutch.
Far too formal, far too bright,
And indoors they're a sorry sight.
Put in a vase they flop and fall
No longer stand up proud and tall.
And someone always tries too much
To breed another "double" Dutch.
So leave them in the fields to grow.
Am I tulip lover? – No!

A Nonsense Rhyme

When the world went 'bong'
And it all went wrong
And the trees turned upside down,
We all felt sad
As the dogs went mad
And the wind blew into town.
So we chopped the trees
In the balmy breeze,
And we watched them all turn brown.
And no one cared,
And no one shared,
In the brand new world of bong
Where the trees were brown
And upside down,
Though we knew that it was wrong.
And we all felt sad
When the dogs went mad
But the birds still sang their song.
So we laughed out loud
But were far too proud
To admit that we'd been wrong.

Tomorrow is Another Day

Tomorrow is another day, thank God!
The dog was sick, the baby screamed.
It turned out worse than I had dreamed.
The car broke down in pouring rain,
I dread a day like this again.
The cleaner broke the oven door
I don't think can take much more.
And just today the boiler broke,
It's really gone beyond a joke.
Tomorrow is another day, thank God!

WAR

Whitehall 2013

I weep for the soldiers all marching,
Row upon row down Whitehall,
Eyes misty with tears of remembrance,
Who long ago answered the call.

For once the sun glints on their medals,
So proudly displayed on their chests,
No raindrops to sully the polish,
So hard won when put to the test.

And my eyes well up too for their memories,
The pain again fresh in their minds,
As they see their friends lost in the battle,
The comrades they all left behind.

So no joy in the laying of poppies,
No joy in the marching of men,
Just gentle and timely reflection,
For November will come round again.

David

That is my brother lying in the trench
His helmet neat beside him
Eyes staring at the sky.
Forgive me, Mother, for I didn't know
That death would come to such as he.
I didn't know of mud and fear and pain.
I only thought of glory and of pride,
Of marching home, a job well done,
With David at my side.
But David lies here now, asleep and cold,
His body broken, never to grow old.
He bade farewell and smiled, and let me go
But yet so peaceful you would never know.

When All Is Said and Done

When all is said and done
Look back upon this day and weep,
For what can we do more?
For broken bodies, blinded eyes,
For shattered limbs and sad, despairing cries;
For brave young men prepared to give their all,
Who left these shores so bright,
Who'd stood so tall.
For all now gone, but to a better place
We must shed tears and wish upon them grace.

The Tower of London 2014

Nine hundred years the walls have stood
And often have they dripped with blood,
And gawping crowds have stopped to stare
At other's pain, as they stood there.
Today they shed red blood again
Reminding us of fresher pain.
Down grey stone walls the poppies flow
Into the yawning moat below,
And spread like blood, across the grass
To halt the breath of we who pass.
Each crimson poppy planted there
A memory of the debt we share.
For once again the crowds have come
To gaze upon what man has done.

After the Battle

Across the field the bugle called
Where all about the bodies lay
And where is all the glory gone
That shone so bright at break of day?

The bloodied earth, now dark with shame
Has formed a blanket for the dead
Who lie at peace beneath the sky
Who'd followed where they all were led.

And far away a mother's cry,
As every mother's cry before,
As yet another soldier sleeps
Amid the mud and death and gore.

But who is left to tell the tale
So many gone just yesterday,
When all the dreams of men have died?
"But that is war," they say.

Retreat

"Retreat, retreat," we'd heard the cry
Yet thought the battle done
But he'd not listened, and instead
Over the top was gone.

I kept beside him, still ahead
When sudden down he fell,
The mud surely a welcome bed
For one who'd lived through hell.

He fell with horror in his eyes
And disbelief at death;
And lonely did I leave him there
Nor wait for his last breath.

"Mother"

Did he think of immortality
As he lay there in the mud?
Or did he cry out for his mother
With his body losing blood?

Did he think he felt the hand of God
As the light went from his eyes?
Or did he cry out for his mother
As he died 'neath foreign skies?

Did he cry out, "Kiss me, Mother,
Once more before I die?"
Did he feel her lips upon his cheek
As she whispered, "Son, goodbye."

The Suitcase

I have a suitcase of memories, which I dare not open.
The straps are tight, the key is locked away.
It is filled with the cries of children;
Of empty faces, dead behind the eyes;
Of burning chimneys;
Broken bodies, heaped upon the dust.
I cannot shut them out.

Yet I know one day I will have to look,
Release the straps and make my peace with God.
For I have hated long and wondered much
How it is possible to find such evil
In the hearts of men.
But I know now I must learn to forgive,
In order to survive.

So when today I hear the cries of children,
Their small, plump faces bright with childhood joy,
The grass is green, the coils of wire are gone,
And fear no longer clutches at my heart.
And I turn back my sleeve
To face at last, the stain upon my skin,
And know I am alive.

SEASONS

September

September, and the dying of the year.
A last defiant shout before the snows,
As green and gold and red in order, turn
The maples, now ablaze with autumn fire.
And damp with early dew the fallen russets
Sit in piles beneath the apple tree.
Ripe, swollen berries, plumped with purple juice
Festoon the silent chapel down the lane,
And hoarfrost crisps the last pink guelder rose.
While in the wood the ancient beeches float
As in a misty dream.
As winter slowly overtakes the land.

Mist

A sad grey mist hangs heavy on the fields,
As bush by bush it creeps across the vale,
Beading bare hedges, dark with winter yet,
With glistening orbs of soft refracted light.
The world is grey, and soft, and still;
Silent as death
Holding its breath to see the winter through.

The Frost Fairy

The frost fairy was out again last night,
Touching the silent earth with her icy fingers;
Flitting unseen beneath a moon so bright
That even the sly brown fox no longer lingers.

She knows that all she touches will be frozen,
That there are those who hate her icy plan.
She only sees the beauty that she's woven
And seeks to make more trouble if she can.

No spider's web nor blade of grass escapes her,
As bush by bush she spreads her fairy scheme.
This mischief-making game is all it takes her
To make the world a white and frozen dream.

Autumn

Russet, crimson, gold,
The colours of fire in a dying world.
Yet look a little closer…

See the hedgehog,
Curled comfortably among the dead leaves,
Building her strength for spring,
Her heartbeat now only five slow beats a minute.
Do not turn the leaves to wake her.

See the fragile spider's web,
Heavy with early-morning dew, suspended miraculously
From one crisp stem to another
The patient, waiting, spider at its centre.
Blow not wind to disturb her.

See the dark hedgerows,
Bright with ripening fruit; rosehip, hawthorn, spindle,
Each crusted now with glistening white hoarfrost,
A feast for hungry birds through the harsh days of winter.
Pick only a few for your table.

See the swallows, gathered together
On the telegraph wires; hear the rustle and chatter,
As they organize themselves
In readiness for the long journey south.
Wish them godspeed for their journey.

Sleep is not death, do not be misled.
The world is simply waiting.
Hold your breath. It will not be long
Until the first snowdrops push up through the frozen earth,
And again it will be spring.

Sun and Moon – A Love Affair

Every night I die a little, as we part.
Alone, you tell me you can breathe again
The cool, perfect air of night.
You need the freedom, I know that,
To be yourself.
And in the dark loneliness of night
I wait.
For dawn, and light, and the opportunity
To be myself again too,
Not just a shadow of you.
Sometimes I catch a pale glimpse of you
As you leave, and I blush,
But still we cannot touch.
We are too different, you and I.
So every night I give you your freedom
And every day you give me mine.
Millennia ago our paths were set.

The North Coast of Denmark

I thought I saw a shooting star last night,
As I stood silent by the shifting sea.
A single streak of iridescent light
Released by Heaven, newly to be free.

And as I watched the comet fall to earth
Beneath a silver moon, I held my breath;
For though I never saw its ancient birth,
I saw its beauty in the throes of death.

Not Knowing

Against a silver sky
The patterns form,
Layer upon layer,
Slowly building.
I watch them, wondering
What they will become
And I wait patiently
Not knowing.

Rain

The gentle rain of evening,
Unexpected.
Wet pavements glisten in the lamplight,
No one talks.
They hasten, silent, hunched against the rain,
Urgently pressed forward,
Dreaming of warmth, and light, and comfort.
A moth, its wings heavy with water,
Staggers beneath the lamplight
Trying to regain its composure.
Only the puddles are still
Beneath the dripping branches,
Blackened and waiting for winter.

Winter

I hold the silence in my hand – waiting.
Waiting for winter to come.
Watching my warm breath clouding the sharp air.
Colder than cold.

A pale moon tracks her path across the Heavens,
Throwing strange shapes upon the darkening land;
Lighting each blade of grass, now white with hoarfrost.
Stiller than still.

And I wait, hardly daring to breathe, knowing it will come,
Until at last the flakes begin to fall
Like petals, in the darkness, layer upon icy layer.
Whiter than white.

The world has been holding its breath tonight.
In the morning it will be a different place;
A land of fairy tales and unimagined dreams.
White, and cold, and beautiful.

Summer

To lie beneath a summer sky
And dream the days as time slips by.
To watch the skylark steeply rise
From earth to Heaven, through azure skies,
And breathe the green of fresh-cut hay,
Touched by the dew of early day.
To hear the blackbird's joyous song
And know 'twill last the summer long.

To spy the blushing rambler rose,
Which through the hedgerow shyly grows,
And hear, amid the apple trees,
The lazy hum of honey bees.
To be reminded, loud and clear,
Of all the things which I hold dear.
As every year its pattern keeps
While in the sun my father sleeps.

LOSS

Do Not Lay Me In a Dark Place

Do not lay me in a dark place
But take me around the world with you.
To see what you have seen,
To bear what you have borne,
To live as you have lived.
Then you may lay me anywhere
And I shall be content

Near Death Experience

Hello. Is anybody there?
I thought St. Peter would be waiting – smiling.
Am I alone, no one to welcome me
Or am I just too soon?
I thought my life complete.
Must I return, to finish what I started?
Is there more still to be done,
More yet to be accomplished,
That I had not seen?

And yet the bright light beckons me
And I would like to go,
To see what lies beyond.
I always wondered how it would be – exactly
Or whether it would 'be' at all.
Until that moment comes no one can say
And then it is too late
To tell those waiting patiently…
And wondering.

Sitting in the Theatre 27 April 2016

Darling Papa, how I miss you.
Suddenly now, here, with no warning,
Tears flow. Don't ask me why.
Did I see a face like yours
Among the crowd? The familiar in a stranger
That stirred a memory?
I cannot say, perhaps.
Time has taught me how to live without you.
I have thought the memories enough
To sustain me. But sometimes, just sometimes,
I long to talk with you.
To hear your voice, to hold your hand,
To hear again your quiet, gentle wisdom,
So familiar, so missed.
Why suddenly, today, here, now,
While people round me sit and eat ice cream
Do I think of you?
See your face, imagine you are with me
And weep hot tears and hope
That no one sees?

I Have Lost My Child

I have lost my child,
No one knows where she has gone.
This morning she smiled at me
And I let her go.
It may be she has been too long with me,
That our allotted spell is done.
Or maybe she chose to go,
Into the wide and empty world, alone
With no one now to hold her hand.
Yet how can I ask her forgiveness
For the freedom that I gave her
And which she took so lightly?
Must I simply say goodbye and never know
What happened to the child I loved so well,
And now is gone?

Download to Oblivion

Is that it?
Is this the end, really,
Of a life lived by the rules?
A small life admittedly
But a happy one, in the main.
I functioned well, I think,
Played my part,
Did as I was told.
Almost always anyway.
Some information not always welcome
But, on the whole,
Honest at least.
Now, in bits and pieces,
My lifetime flickers into squares
Before my eyes.
Are you now just going to turn me off,
Pull out the plug,
Watch the screen go blank,
Say "goodbye", thank you.
You were very useful, until now?
Will that be my epitaph
As I leave this disconnected world
That I have been, admittedly not always willingly,
A part of?

On the Loss of a Child

Could only I be spared the pain
Of love which dwells so deep,
That even I, with open eyes,
Can bear not that you sleep.

Such gentle sleep I should be glad
To say at last, farewell,
And yet I dream of other days
On which I dare not dwell.
When we knew not what lay ahead
Nor even dreamt of tears,
But, had we known, would still be glad
For those few, precious years.

For happy hours of golden sun,
Of pure, unbounded joy,
Of tears and laughter, equal spread,
That measured out each day.
Now all is gone but memory
Yet even now I see
Your smiling face, my perfect child,
But now you are set free.

Free to rejoin the softening earth,
To gaze upon the sky,
To feel the sun upon your face,
For we have said goodbye.

Only the Things I Didn't Do

Only the things I didn't do
Remain to haunt me.
Pieces of life I leave behind,
Unfinished.
The cupboard, dark, untidied
Beneath the stairs.
The pictures still unpainted. Empty canvasses
I had longed to fill.
Music not yet heard,
Books not read; they must be there,
Waiting for me.
The tree, planted too late
To see it touch next summer's sky.
To watch it spread its leafy branches
For the blackbird, whose golden beak
Allows such liquid music.
And yes, the love I leave,
Too soon.
Would that I could have loved more,
For longer.
I would have liked more time
To say goodbye.
So I pick up the pieces, one by one,
And knit them together to make a picture
To take on this final journey.
Small consolation for a life
Half lived.

If I Should Die Tonight

If I should die tonight
Remember how I loved you.
Do not put out the light
Or close the door.
Throw wide the casement window
To the moonlight
That I may watch you still
And love you more.
Love does not die
Because you cannot see me
I am the stars, I am the summer breeze,
I am the early primrose on the hillside,
I am the waves that break upon the shore.
Remember me for all the joy you gave me,
For happiness we shared, a lifetime through,
And in tomorrow's sunshine
You may find me, my footsteps soft
Upon the morning dew.

Friendship Lost

How much do I miss you, when apart?
Friendship is such a gentle art.
I miss you in the silent spring,
When we shared all and everything.
I miss you on the golden days
Of summer, when we used to laze
On grassy banks, beneath the trees,
And share our thoughts with gentle ease.
I miss you on the dying days
Of autumn, with her misty haze.
I miss you in the winter snows,
When something in me colder grows.
For you are gone, we shall no more
Share as we shared so oft before.
Today I weep for friendship lost,
And only now I count the cost.

LIMERICKS

Limerick

There was a young fellow called Dunn,
Who had an affair with a nun.
When she went back to God
With a smile and a nod,
He missed all the heavenly fun.

Limerick

There was a fat man from Tallin,
Who suddenly got very thin.
When his friends asked him why
He replied with a sigh
"It was when I jumped out of my skin."

Limerick

There was a new vicar in Kent,
Who thought what to give up for Lent.
So he gave up his wife
For the rest of his life,
And went off to live in a tent.

Limerick

There was an old lady in France,
Who finally learned how to dance.
She got up on her pointes
And broke all her joints
And wished she'd not taken the chance.

Limerick

There was an old sailor from Mull
Who found life decidedly dull.
So he left in a boat,
Which could only just float
And was left hanging onto the hull.

Limerick

There was a young fellow called Rollo
Whose promises turned out to be hollow.
He promised a lot
Most of which he forgot,
But then promised to do it tomorrow.

MISCELLANEOUS

The Gift

I sit alone, and write,
Pencil on paper, in silence
At my desk.
My father's desk, a lifetime ago.
Words in my head
Seeking freedom, taking shape.
Today perhaps, or tomorrow,
I may let them go.
The words are a gift,
From somewhere.
In the genes maybe?
And in turn they are my gift to you,
For what they are worth,
If anything.
I write
Because I cannot help myself.

Waiting at the Eurostar Terminus

Machines whirr as the people pass,
Who wonders where they go?
Excitement ruling hasty steps,
Who interrupts the flow?

From here to there, and back again,
With no time in-between:
Another place, another land,
To countries yet unseen.

No one has time to take it in,
The passage oh so brief,
A breakfast here, a dinner there
Oh, time is such a thief!

The fault is ours, we should have known,
For we have built this place
And through the air and on the sea
All life is now a race.

And we care not, but should have learned,
That time is what we need.
And yet we listen not it seems,
Ruled only by our greed.

1963

There was a time there was a boy,
When life seemed true and full of joy.
Music and colour, love and light
Were all it took to make life bright.
"We'll march to show the world we care,
We'll wear no clothes and grow our hair."
"We'll ban the bomb and make world peace,
We'll show them all that war can cease."
"We'll change the world from bad to good."

―――

Or did we only think we could?

Despair 1750

A lumpy woman, slumped, laughing,
Upon a doorstep.
Not drunk, exactly,
But neither is she sober.
Voluminous layers of clothing,
Ragged, grey,
Tied up haphazardly
With string.
Loose woollen stockings,
With holes;
And shoes; muddy, laceless,
Brown-ish.
A cotton bonnet, ribbons untied.
And a child,
Upon an empty breast,
Crying dirty tears.
The stench of gin, and despair
Like a halo.
And beside her on the steps
An empty china bottle.

Despair 2020

A youngish man,
Well, not exactly young,
But not old either.
Asleep maybe – or not,
Difficult to tell.
A sheet of card beneath him
On the pavement,
Neatly folded – damp.
Small coins,
Not many, not enough,
In a cardboard cup, from Costa.
A blanket, slightly torn,
With blue stripes.
A gift perhaps
Wrapped tightly round his body.
Beside him, a large untidy dog,
Snoring.
And at his feet
An empty plastic bottle.

Good God!

I can't quite let you go.
Yet neither can I believe
That you are there,
For you do nothing.
How can you just stand by
And watch
The horrors of the world?
Where is the justice?
What are you doing
While neighbour fights next door neighbour,
And people die of hunger and disease?
While children lie and bleed
Upon the dust?
I do not understand you.
This is your world, you have made it.
Have you no pity?
Do you not hear our helpless cries of despair,
As we link hands around the earth
For what it might have been?

Stranger Danger

A stranger asked me out for tea
But that didn't allow him to be so free,
So I quickly removed his hand from my knee.

To be quite honest I really don't see
Just how insensitive you can be
With a girl you've only asked out for tea.

But on that we clearly didn't agree,
So when he tried again, (with inordinate glee)
I picked up my bag and decided to flee.

I Am Called to the Sea

I am called to the sea
And the lonely cry of the gulls.
And the boats along the quayside
With their battered, rusting hulls.
And the rattle of the shingle
As the water pulls away.
And the singing in the rigging
'Neath a sky of leaden grey.
And the wailing of the foghorn,
And the sighing of the deep,
As the mist creeps up the shoreline,
Swirling round the ancient keep.
And the rugged, time-worn sailors
With their weathered, salt-scorched skin,
And the vastness of the ocean
As they haul their catches in.
Long gone are the days when I yearn to be free,
As, year after year, I am called to the sea.

Fear

I cannot open the door.
My hand is on the catch,
But courage fails me.
I am paralysed by fear,
My mouth so dry I cannot swallow.
Rivers of sweat collect
Upon my skin.
My heart thuds,
Hard enough to split my chest.
The pain is palpable.
Outside, the busy world, so full of life,
Still beckons me.
I long to join in.
Tomorrow I will try again.

Waiting

I sit and watch – and wait,
As all the world goes by.
The pulse of life
Passing by my window.
No one notices.
I am a stranger now
To the outside world.
I have not been there
Recently.
Soon she will come,
She always does.
Eleven o'clock prompt.
She will come with a smile
"Hello Mrs. Walker, how are we today?"
"Good morning, Mary,
We are fine, thank you."
"We"? Who are "we"?
Am I no longer Janet?
Am I no longer anybody?
And yet I do wait, look forward even,
To her smile, her optimistic voice,
Familiar.
And while I wait
The world outside rolls on
And no one sees me by my window
Waiting…

Tell Me the Truth

Tell me the truth about living.
Is it full of fresh wonder anew
That is talked about all the world over
Yet searched for and found by so few?

Is it something so special, elusive,
That those who have found it are rare?
Is it something completely exclusive
Or something we all need to share?

If I find it, then how can I keep it
And spread the good news to my friends?
Can I box it up neatly with ribbons
To make certain the joy never ends?

On First Hearing Mahler's Symphony No. 5

Such utter, utter beauty.
It haunts the muted hollows of my soul,
Tears me apart,
Brings tears of love and joy,
Or utter desperation.
Does it cost so much to write
I wonder?
Was the composer too, torn apart,
In the writing?
In the precise arrangement
Of the notes upon the lines?
And when he heard it,
For the first time, complete,
Was it how he imagined it to be?
Did he know that it would make me weep
Or catch my breath in wonder?
He surely must have done,
For selfish would be he
Who wrote it only for himself.

Mermaids

As I lay sleeping on the rocky shore
I dreamed of mermaids tumbling in the waves,
Their tinkling laughter breaking the night air,
Their bodies milky white beneath the moon.
They wore pearl earrings plucked from oyster shells,
And stranded necklaces of waving coral.
"We know of a man," they sing
"Who weeps upon the shore.
He is weeping for his love, but she is gone.
If he would come with us beneath the waves
No longer would he weep for his lost love.
But he must know he never can return,
He will become a creature of the sea
And we will hold him fast."
And in my dream I heard them call my name
"Come with us," they cried, "play with us.
We have palaces beneath the waves
And gardens made from brightly coloured coral.
The songs of whales will lull you into slumber,
On beds of golden sand."
So nearly did I go with them, to seek oblivion.
But in a sudden moment they were gone,
Vanished beneath the waves,
Tails flashing silver in the briny foam.
And when at last I woke, a single pearl
Lay on the mossy rock where I had slept.

Where I Belong

I don't really live here. This house isn't mine
It belongs to a friend.
The debris of unhappiness is all around me.
"Please use it while I'm away.
I need a break. I need time to think.
Pretend it's yours, just for a few days."

And it's not mine. I'm a tidy person,
Contented in my life.
But somehow I like it here,
Perhaps because I'm only here for a while.
I like the fact that I don't have to think,
About anything.
There is nothing for me to do here.
I am free.

But at home, my home, my family waits.
The husband who loves me, and misses me.
The children who love me too – sometimes.
They look forward to my return,
To the place where I pick up the pieces of my life again,
And where I really belong.

Analysis of Friendship

I cannot tell what holds us together.
If I try to analyse it I am lost.
Too deep by far, to explain
To outsiders, who will never understand
What binds us.
In part it is memory, shared experience;
In part a common union of values.
Years back, when we first met
I do not remember how it was,
But since then we have always been together.
Except of course, in love.
And there we have to disagree.
We each have love, but love sets us apart.
Our friendship is not changed,
But now we have to take more care,
And it is no longer quite the same.

?

So far from hope, it was despair,
I know not what had brought me there.

I only know that for a while,
I found I could no longer smile.

No longer smile at life's sweet path,
Nor find within it any worth.

It maybe was the loss of love,
That left me where I could not move.

And then one day, amid the pain
I sought to find the light again.

And found it had been always there
And learned again to trust and care.

I Am Afraid of the Night

I am afraid of the night,
Of the lonely darkness
Creeping through my window.
Of the hooting owl
On silent wings, who passes,
Fear keeps me from sleep.
The shadows in my room,
So familiar in daylight,
Are no longer my friends.
The night sounds startle me.
Each leafy rustle
Of the furtive hedgehog
A warning somehow,
But of what, I do not know.
A cracking branch
Beneath a careless foot
Makes me leap from my pillow,
Alert, eyes wide, ready to run.
Yet I know that I am foolish
And that with the dawn
All terror will be gone.

Coronavirus

I know you are out there – waiting
To catch me unawares.
Biding your time, choosing your moment
To strike,
Sometime in the future.
You have become crazed with power,
Gained strength, spread fear.
You think you can do anything
And I have fallen, unwittingly,
Into your trap.
I will not let you bend me
To your will. Instead
I will look to the beautiful things
You cannot destroy:
Sunlight upon water, butterflies,
Stars hanging in a midnight sky.
I know you are out there – waiting
But I will not listen to you, anymore.

Has Anybody Seen My Mind?

Has anybody seen my mind?
I know I had it yesterday.
I had it when I made the lunch
And then it seemed to go away.

And after lunch I walked the dog,
I had it then, I feel quite sure.
Then suddenly it went again
I really wish I had it more.

It happens several times a day
And causes somehow so much pain.
I never quite know where I am
Or when it will come back again.

They say there's medication now,
I'm worried that may be a lie
And wonder will it be like this
Forever now, until I die.

Christmas 2020

Christmas will not be the same this year.
No Christmas table laden, full of cheer,
No holly berries red, or scented pine
Upon the mantle where no candles shine.
Fresh ivy does not trail from stair to stair
Nor Father Christmas sleep in the armchair.
No parcels piled beneath the Christmas tree,
No happy laughter fills the house with glee.
No turkey, Christmas pudding, no mince pies.
No brandy butter, crackers to surprise.
No carol singers outside in the gloom
Their joyous voices filling every room.
So in the end it's just another day
For what coronavirus took away.

After Dickens

"Did'st thou sleep well last night?"
"Oh no, not I. So wide awake and restless did I lie.
On such a night Saint Nicholas may come
Laden with toys and sweetmeats for the poor.
If I should sleep and he knock on the door
He would not tarry on so cold a night,
But travel on where he'd be welcome more:
Where children lie abed and dream in vain
Of larders, bare of victuals, full again:
Of turkey and plum pudding, sweet mince pies,
Such riches as would widen children's eyes.
Where hearths are warm and coals are glowing bright
On upturned faces in the candlelight.
Where dreams are dreams, yet hope holds fast
For this is what we know,
For this one night, this one alone, a single star did glow
High in the distant heavens upon those here below.
Where wise men know that dreams are dreams
Yet followed still a star,
That told of unknown mysteries,
A Christ-child from afar.
Thus every child is laid down with a kiss,
So great is love, on such a night as this.

"Forbidden"

I should have said "no," straight away.
It should have been easy.
But instead I took the bowl – and drank.
You had warned me, before I left
"If they give you Peyote say 'no'"
But I knew better, of course.
I always do.
And so, in order not to seem a fool I suppose,
I drank it.
Please don't say "I told you so."
What happened next
Is unbelievable.
I threw up,
The world spun,
The whole jungle seemed to be screaming.
I was blinded with colour.
Colours I have never seen before,
Colours that danced,
Colours that don't exist.
Strange creatures came and went.
The trees were alive,
Their branches whipping around me
Binding me tight.
I was unable to move – paralysed.
All night I fought
And howled to the sky.

In the morning the jungle was quiet,
The tribe going about its everyday business.
As I lay on my bed the children watched,
Taking turns, wide-eyed
"The Englishman" and laughing.
But no one was surprised.
Apparently this was normal, cleansing,
Anticipated.
As was the headache
Which split my head in two
For the next three days and nights.

"Oh Come All Ye Faithfull"

Every Sunday they come,
Dressed up to the nines,
Clutching recalcitrant children
By the hand.
Setting an example,
Smiling and chatting,
Filled with goodwill
To all men.
Their voices rise to the ancient rafters,
As they have done
For millennia.
But the words no longer have meaning.
Too familiar to have value
After all this time.
Replaced instead
By a hundred everyday thoughts.
The vicar intones about love,
And hope, and compassion.
They think of the Sunday roast.
Did they turn on the oven?
Lock the front door?
Let out the cat?
At the end, still smiling,
Their generous purses
Fill the waiting collection plates,
Easing their conscience,
Doing their bit.
They do not see that God
Lies dead before the alter.

Belonging

I do not belong here,
I am different from you.
You welcome me with open arms,
Yet I do not feel at home.
I see the tension in your face
When we shake hands.
When you see me in the street
You stare a little.
Not unkindly perhaps, but I notice.
Today you smiled at me
When others turned away
And I was grateful
But still I sensed your hesitation.
Yet are we not essentially the same
You and I?
Do we not love and hate?
Do we not share the same dreams
For our future?
I have tried so hard to belong
To take your English customs as my own,
But it isn't always easy,
And I am aware of every contradiction.
Could we not start again?
Otherwise I will always be a stranger.

A Storm

Fear, like a beacon, shines from your frightened eyes
When thunder rolls and lightening splits the skies.
When you were small you'd hide deep in your bed
And pull the covers high above your head.
I'd take you up but could not make you see
The wonder that a storm presents to me.
And so I'd hold you tight against my breast
Until the thunder stopped and you could rest.

The Man I Used To Be

I can almost touch it,
The life I had,
The man I used to be.
Today my daughter comes, smiling,
With open arms.
"I love you, Papa. We're walking today
Across the field again.
You remember, Papa
We walked there yesterday?
You lost your stick.
Today we can cut you a new one."
The field is cool, and green,
But unfamiliar.
The sky is blue,
There are cotton-wool clouds and daisies.
Children are running and shouting,
It is beautiful.
I had forgotten beauty.
I hesitate,
She takes my arm.
"Come on, Papa. Only a little bit further
And then we can go home."
Behind us she turns to shut the gate
And we cross the road.
As we part she hugs me
And I remember it all.

The Devil You Know

I am waiting for Professor Dunn,
The man who tests my eyes.
Recently they have been fine,
But there is a devil there
Waiting with me too.
The devil and I wait together
We are old friends now.
It could be tomorrow,
Or next year.
If I am lucky, even longer.
But one day the devil will come
And my eyes will no longer be
The old, familiar friends
I can rely on.
How strange to know that it will happen,
But not when.
And when he does come, Professor Dunn
He will tell me what I already know.
But he will tell me kindly, with a smile,
And I will thank him, shake his hand
And the devil and I will leave together
To follow the broad green line
On the pavement
Back to Old Street Station.

When I Write in the Night

I am a hostage to the night
It holds me fast.
Silent lines in my head
Wait for freedom.
Words tumble, uninvited,
They leap and dance,
I rearrange them,
Set them out,
Tell them how to behave.
But they have a life of their own
Their ending is not mine.
They have chosen another way,
It happens.
And I follow as I must
So that sometimes even I am confused.

Acknowledgements

My thanks to Harriet Grace, who managed to convince me that other people may want to read what I write and to SilverWood Books, especially Catherine, for their unstinting patience with my reluctant use of technology.

Lightning Source UK Ltd.
Milton Keynes UK
UKHW040041010223
416273UK00001B/63